NECESSITIES

ALSO BY CHRISTOPHER MERRILL

Workbook (poems)

Outcroppings: John McPhee in the West (editor)

Fevers & Tides (poems)

The Forgotten Language: Contemporary Poets and Nature (editor)

From the Faraway Nearby: Georgia O'Keeffe as Icon (editor, with Ellen Bradbury)

The Grass of Another Country: A Journey Through the World of Soccer (nonfiction)

Anxious Moments, prose poems by Aleš Debeljak (translator, with the author)

Watch Fire (poems)

What Will Suffice: Contemporary American Poets on the Art of Poetry (editor, with Christopher Buckley)

The Old Bridge: The Third Balkan War and the Age of the Refugee (nonfiction)

The Forest of Speaking Trees: An Essay on Poetry

Your Final Pleasure: An Essay on Reading

The Four Questions of Melancholy: New and Selected Poems of Tomaž Šalamun (editor)

The Way to the Salt Marsh: A John Hay Reader (editor)

The City and the Child, poems by Aleš Debeljak (translator, with the author)

Only the Nails Remain: Scenes from the Balkan Wars (nonfiction)

Brilliant Water (poems)

Things of the Hidden God: Journey to the Holy Mountain (nonfiction)

Even Birds Leave the World: Selected Poems of Ji-woo Huang (translator, with Won-Chung Kim)

Because of the Rain: A Selection of Korean Zen Poems (translator, with Won-Chung Kim)

Scale and Stairs: Selected Poems of Heeduk Ra (translator, with Won-Chung Kim)

7 Poets, 4 Days, 1 Book (collaborative poem, with Marvin Bell, István László Geher, Ksenia Golubovich, Simone Inguanez, Tomaž Šalamun, and Dean Young)

Translucency: Selected Poems of Chankyung Sung (translator, with Won-Chung Kim)

The Tree of the Doves: Ceremony, Expedition, War (nonfiction)

The New Symposium: Poets and Writers on What We Hold in Common (editor, with Nataša Ďurovičová)

The Growth of a Shadow: Selected Poems of Taejoon Moon (translator, with Won-Chung Kim)

NECESSITIES

CHRISTOPHER MERRILL

WHITE PINE PRESS / BUFFALO, NEW YORK

WHITE PINE PRESS
P.O. Box 236
BUFFALO, NEW YORK 14201
www.whitepine.org

ACKNOWLEDGMENTS

I am very grateful to the editors of *The American Poetry Review, Field, jubilat, Notre Dame Review, The Prose Poem: An International Journal*, and *Sentence: A Journal of Prose Poetics*, in which some of these poems were first published.

Publication of this book was made possible, in part, by grants from
the National Endowment for the Arts, which believes that a great nation deserves great art;
with public funds from the New York State Council on the Arts, a State Agency;
and with support from the Office of the Vice President for Research at the University of Iowa.

First Edition.

ISBN: 978-1-935210-46-7

Printed and bound in the United States of America.

Library of Congress Control Number: 2012948068

Necessity knows no rules.
                                    —Primo Levi

*I wanted to know what was helpless in my behavior—
how I would behave out of necessity.*
                                    —Jasper Johns

Necessity is the veil of God.
                                    —Simone Weil

It was either an abandoned coffeehouse or *The Pharmacy of God*—the hovel into which we had stumbled in the dark. On the shelves were nails pried from crosses in the desert, glass bottles named *The Beginning* and *The End*, bandages stolen from the wounded at Ardennes. Our spirit of adventure was a flag no one waved. What was helpless in our behavior, central to our design? The common rituals: pressing cider in a barn fire, tracking bears around the zoo, howling at the cats decapitated by coyotes. Blues singers were stripping paint off the signs in the beer halls. At twilight, animal trainers sailed down the burning river in a barge, the first chapters of aborted novels stuffed in their pockets; their wives, dressed in skirts fringed with mink, were too shy to mention the smoke rising around them. These were characters without character, not mirrors of our regret. Nor are we exiles in this backwater: we're the deputies keeping watch.

Who are these heroes pinned to the ceiling of the den? Do they know the thieves locked in the bathroom, the pirates writing prescriptions for the spirit—which is smaller than we think? The saint carrying wood into the storeroom fears the black widows and scorpions searching for a warm place to winter. Shelter is the language we're learning, the *bella lingua* of the ferryman lurching out of the bar. High winds and waves, the promise of a new beginning, Americas on every page: who will write the next constitution, the next declaration of individuality? Certainly not the heroes who hiked into the mountains one morning to discover the spring was poisoned, the oracle silent, and the order of fountain pens still on a loading dock by the burning river. And the thieves—the thieves are afflicted with ringing in their ears: each hears the same singer wailing at the top of her voice, warning him to sail away before the saint returns.

The saint's arms are chafed and strong from carrying the same bundle of wood he was given the day he entered the order. He leaves trails of sawdust in the monastery and the apple orchard; the messages he delivers to the thieves keeping watch over the storeroom are hieroglyphs to him—he never learned to read. *Who can understand the handwriting of the spirits?* he sometimes asks the thieves, who never laugh at his jokes. Nails, rusted nails, are what he collects. His favorite word is *America*, although the cider they make there, he likes to tell the thieves, is inferior to the ancient wines his friend the ferryman imports from Mongolia. Remember when the horses galloped through the orchard, through the falling snow? A posse was heading for the hills: why they wanted to gut-shoot the wild mustangs was anybody's guess. *Put the game warden to sleep!* the saint will cry the night he gives his nails to the thieves, praying they will follow him.

Return the swastikas—that's what the letter instructed us to do. No signature. The canceled stamp bore the figure of a famous poet. The thieves thought our confusion was a mask. Yet they offered to forge new documents for us. Our passports had expired, and we were afraid to ride our horses over the Alps—the Trinity Alps, that is, where vigilantes had turned the saw mills into training centers for the afterlife. The felled trees spiked with nails, tribes drowned in the lake, rugs woven out of feathers: these we could return, at least in theory. *Where's the poet?* we asked the thieves, who were printing up a series of manifestoes concerning the rights of bears. We had run out of fences. Feathers, too. The horses lay on the ground, in the first snow of the season. We propped a cross against the barn door and bolted it shut. We vowed not to open our mail until the spring runoff, when we could present our credentials to the guards at the pass.

Fictions and masks and swastikas. We saw the tribesmen gathering on the ridge. Then they were gone. In the course of the fire raging by the river, in the scat singing of the women in the streets, in the false trails the bears made to trick us into following them, even in the saint's digressions—in everything there was a thread to wind into a skein, into a language and a style. Leaves fell like syllables from the tongues of rocking congregations, in tents all over America. The horses stayed behind, the walls shook. The ground was a long wave studded with flags, like buoys. No one could read the charts; the maps of our despair were useless. And the visas counterfeited by the thieves would not have fooled anyone. So we planned to winter in the mountains, in a style appropriate to the age: in hair shirts and tiaras, with halberds and tracts detailing the spiritual exercises of our enemies. Our masks and fictions we would save for the summer solstice.

How could we have known the bridge was closed? We had the wrong tools for fixing or framing a burning river; our stamps did not impress the ferryman. Nor did we recognize the poet waving a flag at his despair, the recruits marching in lock step over the mountain. The proclamations of the one-armed sawyers had no impact on the number of trees hauled to the mill. *Who's singing?* the thieves asked. Bells rang in every barn, where coyotes roamed and the water troughs had frozen over. Skate home, if you think you can find ice thick enough to table discussion of the proposed rule changes until the next meeting. And don't forget to write thank-you notes to the survivors of the earthquake and the fire. Tell them they should have listened to the bears, not the saint. For there are swastikas yet to burn. And the river, the language of fire and ice, is rising faster than we imagined. If only we had called the bridgetender before we sent for you!

Only gestures will help us now: melting wax on the wood stove, perfuming the air to cut short the dinner party; smuggling sentences from *The Story of O* into tour guides of the Caribbean; teaching bachelors to pan for gold. No sense in dictating instructions to the overpopulated past: they never listen. Is that musk you're wearing? Or a mask of the future? Let me count to fifty, then I'll come looking for you. Don't hide behind a tree. Hunting season has been extended indefinitely, and I have three words locked in a safe, none of which will function as a balm when the temperature drops below freezing. I also have strings of salt hanging from the rafters, a knife made out of staghorn to gut the albino deer framed in our sights, and enough chili powder to blister the tongue of a hasty reader. That note was for your eyes only: why did you show it to the guide? How can you speak to the protesters in such a reassuring manner? Where are you going?

Every building from the century of costume balls must be razed, according to the professors of desire, the men in top hats writing letters of recommendation for their versions of the past. The wooden matches they produce will never light the stove or end an argument, though the water leaking from the canisters in the salt caverns should clear our minds: every marksman can see the river glowing at dusk. *Razed* or *raised?* These are terms for the initiated. But no one will go hungry tonight, at least not in the canyons patrolled by coyotes. Fill the wine glasses with Apache tears, hard and black as the forgotten histories of America: we would use them as instruments of writing or torture, if we weren't afraid of the dark. Nor can we console the woman crying by the stove; the dress she bought at an estate auction is stained with blood. *Besides,* say the professors passing their top hats out the window, *it's too cold to wear a sun dress to the ball.*

Reinvent the past: that was how the patent lawyers proposed to solve the housing shortage. Resurrect the sonnet and symposium, crossbow and convent. They filled prescription pads with demolition orders for the illiterate. They watched the river burn. The drunken ferryman suspended crossings in calm weather. No passengers complained when the inventors, who worked in their sleep, promised to march with the homeless, whose protest was in its seventh year. The ground shook. Bridges crumpled like paper. A cry rose up from the stock exchange: *Sell today, or jump tomorrow!* The futures market had closed early, the fire having spread from the mouth of the river into the songs of the women in the street. No one said a word about the man carrying a rifle into the patent office: he looked like any other soldier of fortune. Even when he took aim at us we held our tongues. Sunlight streamed through the window. We smelled smoke.

Words borne across the land—by wind, in glacial drift, along the meandering course of the burning river: is that the reclining poet, the stick figure by the barn? Why is the horse eating paint? And who is imprisoned in *The Red Tower*—the artist or the viewer? We had more than enough answers to go around, yet we failed every test administered by the military authorities. And when night raised its flags we saluted the dark. History, that is—the way a cairn is raised above the river and by morning charred rocks are scattered across thousands of pages. The white horse circled the tower. *Faster, faster!* commanded the dog-sled driver from Nome, though the snow had long since melted. His huskies refused to pull the sled laden with dictionaries through the wildflower meadow, over wheel ruts and rusted traps and rocks left by the retreating glacier. But that was where we hoped to learn the local language, if we could find a native speaker.

Dust off the words collected from the broken printing press, then stuff the extra type in the parking meters on the barricaded street, where the homeless are on the march again. They avoid the bicycle messenger, the boy with a hatful of theories about the lovers hiding in the orchard. He spends his lunch hour at the zoo, taunting the bear that bangs its head against the bars of its cage—anything to escape the whistle of the train that never arrives! The street is emptying, and the police can't keep up with the thieves who have keys to the meters. The mirrors in the judges' chambers are cracked, reinforcing the saint's argument that government is blind. *Mercy* is a word to hoard, the saint says, like leaves for the garden, now that the fertilizer factory is closing down. His last message to the lovers was not delivered: *The Puritans are coming!* That's why the apple pickers won't work—and why the poor are heading for the zoo. The bear roars at the smiling boy.

No one checked the traps by the river. So the wolves and coyotes caught in the iron claws howled at the sun, gnawing on their flesh to free themselves. Was that the mask you knew us by? We had our list of names to offer to the authorities, places to hide, a cache of food. The hermit climbing toward the ridge was in our sights; the earplugs stolen from the army depot protected us from the voices we could not identify, which were either in the walls or just outside the window: cries of animals, evacuation orders, homilies on the Last Judgment. Even the greediest trappers had found lovers in the city; nothing could convince them to canoe the burning river, not even when the barricades went up. At nightfall, when the hermit took in a three-legged wolf, we realized you had seen through our disguise. We had to act fast: our list was growing longer, our supplies were dwindling, and no one knew how to fire a gun. There were voices everywhere.

The theater had closed for the winter. Yet there was a line outside the ticket window—old men in combat fatigues, women nursing wolves on the verge of extinction, children prepared to march against anything. Street cleaners and chimney sweeps were hard at work, though all the cars had been stripped, the shops and houses boarded up or burned. We had left our maps at the asylum, surprised by the patients' interest in cartography: they wanted directions to the Trinity Alps and walk-on parts in the filming of the Last Judgment. But our vial of nerve gas was intact; the guns distributed by the government during the election we had hidden before fleeing to the mountains, where the caldera had been fenced in since our last escape. A herd of cattle circled the crater, smoke drifted through the trees, and behind the barbed wire soldiers were counting off our names. We hurried after the procession of hired mourners filing into the camp.

The blacksmith speaks in tongues to settle the horse that kicked him in the head, the white mare that he must shoe before the exodus begins. The metal plate in his skull functions as a lightning rod for the church; his congregation thinks the rusted nails he uses once belonged to a saint. But no shoes fit; the fire keeps burning out; and the horse's owner, who paid in knives last time, did not enclose enough pennies to ward off bad luck. The boatload of refugees who drifted out to sea, believing the new anchor would catch, returns to port. *A word is a rudder and a sail,* the blacksmith sings. *Where will we sleep tonight?* they ask. He tells them his dream: to forge a currency out of alms and intrigue. The horse is impatient. And the faithful march to the paddock, scanning the sky for thunderheads. In the barn is a cross soaking in gasoline: if the blacksmith's luck changes, one spark from his anvil will ignite another wave of conversions.

The minister was replaced when the congregation discovered Hell's hierarchies. They could no longer ignore his praise for the storm clouds on the horizon, they blamed him for the way the sea ate into the coastline, they didn't believe his claim of owning shares in *The Pharmacy of God*. Even his pitch for the after-life—*The best prices in Mexico!*—proved false: he had never been to Mexico. Nor did they trust his map of the heavens, his need to put everything in parentheses: the sky was not an (interlude) for the faithful. But it was a good time for those who recognized the danger of translating allegory into a modern idiom: each choice in favor of contemporary diction and syntax represented the sacrifice of another division of angels—impossible to consider until the campaign against miracle plays had ended. *Perhaps we should leave it (the story, the sea) in the original?* the new minister suggested. The congregation listened closely.

The city was sinking, and the burning river rose higher than anyone imagined. If only we could understand the chanting in the cathedral! Or find enough ink to write constitutions for the animals in the zoo and penal codes for the plants in the botanical garden! Or remember where we hid the life jackets, the ashes of the oars we burned in the rowboats, the moorings you knew us by! We had not discovered a new route to Juárez, the Lost City of Gold! Smoke straddled the border—it was impossible to breathe—yet the streets were lined with trumpeters and white swans. *Are we there yet?* asked the men clutching demolition orders. No one kept watch over the bridge, and when the chanting turned into a battle cry fire flowed down the side streets, torching cars and the proclamations nailed to the doors of the animal trainers. Ashes, feathers, and music filled the air. If only we could learn what happened to the gold buried at the border!

Cloistered in fire, in the snow-covered desert, in the crab apples rotting in the monk's cell: Why did you abandon us during the service? Where did you hide the stamps the soldiers left on the altar? Who will be your second? This is an event not to miss—*a marriage of convulsions*, says the saint who took over the kitchen after the last skirmish. The floor is a spill of blood and feathers. The message entrusted to the deaf boy will never arrive. And the soldiers refuse to tell us who they buried on the mesa. But each rock of the cairn is a signed confession, which will remain sealed until we find a place to store our summer clothes, our ancestors' erotica. The message? *Don't let the roots dry out!* Time to assemble a new field guide for lovers, to shore up the walls of the courtyard in which we used to duel. Coyotes are digging around the cairn. The saint is cooking enough geese for an army. The monk burns all our mail. Smoke rises from the snow.

Masks, monuments, mildew. What nourishes exile once the leaves begin to fall? Our windows were broken so often they can't be closed, and the weight training in our apprenticeship left us muscle-bound—hypersensitive, that is, to sunlight. Open the trunk before the moths escape across the border, then light a candle for the partisans in the woods. The myth we live by now bears no relation to the books we burned last month. The fine ash drifting down from the sky? We'll wear it to the costume ball, the invitations to which were never mailed. No wonder the papers say that government is blind! The pack of Seeing Eye dogs circling the Virgin's shrine (O Love!) won't find the partisans armed with rocks. And if we strip by the window? Shield your eyes: the traffic patterns near the guildhall may change, but the glare from the shrine makes it impossible to read the books on the pyre. Nothing can stop the moths, the leaves, the exodus.

They found us in the storeroom, picking over the crab apples. Starving, unarmed, we had never learned the word for *history* in their language, so we invented a theology based on our journey up the frozen river: how our bloodied skates gleamed in the torchlight, how we came to distrust our ancestors' clocks and catapults. We hid the compass in the bin, then raised our hands, certain we could answer any question: a martyr's name, the date of an arctic voyage, our favorite version of *Smoke Gets in Your Eyes*. Our faith in criticism, in exile, had forced us to act without thinking: if only we had checked the tomatoes ripening in the paper bag! But we were tired of the drunken musicians in our homeland, we wanted something pure. And our captors had forgotten to lock the door. *Attention!* they cried in three different languages, none of which we scorned. When they blindfolded us, we smelled smoke. A clock ticked. The compass pointed toward the sky.

The foundation had rotted, and the timbers propping up the house splintered into cults, whose chief attraction was the promise of wealth. After the harvest, the migrant workers hauled buckets of dirt from the cellar and rubbed it into their chests, praying for the solar flares to end. They suffered from heartburn, too. They regretted sending their families to the interior. Our paramour was a world governed by the Furies. Worms circled the apple the scribe kept in his desk to remind him of his fate, the way monks sleep in their coffins. The water supply was tainted, and we had no rules to fall back on. Woodcutters shelled the trees marked for the mill. The helicopter summoned to evacuate the dying couldn't land. And who would dare to slaughter the last lamb to appease you? The sun was brighter yet. Someone offered to write a new prayer. The dirt—all that held the house in place—was so contaminated we told the migrants to wear masks.

Blame it on the scimitars, not the scientific method, we told the professors after setting the field ablaze with a magnifying glass. Yet the signs posted by the farmer, warning hunters about the canisters of toxic waste buried on his land, frightened us. It was elk season, the buglers' busiest time: we kept mistaking taps for mating calls. What had we bagged? A bicycle and a bear. The newspapers printed photographs of famous lovers to clear up our confusion. Nothing helped. The field resembled an ammunition dump—one explosion after another. We had to conduct our studies elsewhere, if we hoped to keep our thesis secret while we followed the tracks to a cave in the mountains. Our prey was either language or style, it was too soon to decide which. A drummer beat time at the edge of the burning field. Thousands of soldiers shadowboxed with their mistresses. The professors sharpened their swords. We moved in to take a closer look.

The print's a fake, the guard assured us, winking at the woman in the blue sari. *Starry Night?* We were waiting for the press conference to begin, when the museum would unveil the latest scandal, our investigation into the woman's role in the curator's downfall having left us vulnerable to her charms. *She's no Hindu,* we declared, checking our money belts. But our search for *The Pharmacy of God* had turned up nothing, and at the private auction, where we had our eye on the afterlife, we were advised to repent for leaving our weapons in the mountains. Hence our pilgrimage to the museum. The photographers and critics formed a circle around the woman in blue, who knelt in prayer. Everyone agreed that her print was more beautiful than the original. What it lacked was a title. *Pietà?* said the guard. *Who will open the bidding?* said the duped curator, winking at the woman. We had more targets than money, but our aim was improving.

Shoot the horse—that's what the blacksmith thinks, limping to his truck. The white mare tied to the apple tree rises on its hind legs, parting the waves of blood, stubble, and fallen fruit. The frost is a stained glass window giving on to the future. Giving? It takes from the past, which includes last night's clouds, this morning's argument over the clergy's role in politics, and what caught the blacksmith's attention just before he was kicked. Only the rope tethering the mare belongs to the present, and it—the rope, the present—is fraying at both ends. Likewise the blacksmith's nerves: his followers, awaiting his instructions, stand at the edge of a sea that dried up long ago. Yet we shield our eyes when the priest in the prompter's box shouts: *Too many actors in the capital!* He's the stage manager of a bankrupt theater, he believes in nothing—not the Epiphany, nor the afterlife, nor even the most obvious signs of stagecraft in the shaping of our destiny:

abandoned cities; dying forests and lakes; histrionics in *The Pharmacy of God*. Winter figures into one of the priest's cues or equations, although he can't remember why. Nor can we explain our elation over the canceled elections. Give the blacksmith something besides a pistol for his pain, and then take from him all the spiritual choices arriving in glass coaches at dusk, which overwhelm us with kindness. Where should we look for the stone tablets? Will they mention the horse and tree? Which window should we open tonight? And the sea—what happened to the sea? These questions we should have answered before the lights dimmed. The curtains rise on an empty stage. The clouds in the backdrop resemble cassocks. And the actors in the wings will never finish the penal code, or lead us out of the temptation to forget the past, or organize the exodus across the desert. The rope's about to break: there will be no more dress rehearsals.

II

When we couldn't find an open window, we decided to climb back up the mountain to retrieve our knives, our style. But our maps were covered with typographical errors: Kenya was Cain; Albania, Abel. And the mapmakers hiding in the woods, clutching copies of the Dead Sea Scrolls, wondered what to do with Montana. Moses? It was enough to exhaust our emotional reserves.

Our wine cellars, too. Even the creek had run dry, despite the warning signs posted near the poisoned spring. We were tempted to set fire to the withered grass and steal the rolls of barbed wire the fencing company had left at the foot of the mountain. Better to stake out our domain (dusk and dawn) in the Kingdom of Chance than follow signs corresponding to patterns of belief we no longer understood. For it was too late to mount another expedition to the Black Sea.

We were of two minds: to find a cure for lockjaw or learn sign language. *Are these the Balkan Mountains?* we sang to scare the mapmakers. *Or are we on our way to Babylon?* Our tongues burned, and the blacksmith's tongs hissed at the snakes sunning themselves by the creek. Windows closed around us, like dancers circling a virgin prepared for sacrifice—the naked woman twisting on a litter of teak, eyes fixed on the altar and the glinting knives of the priests...

Then we remembered the museum guard's warning not to return the wine and ancient texts we had stolen for the mapmakers. But he had said nothing about the library sending us truckloads of books—so many books we had to flee to the caves in which the hermits, the Great Invisibles, wrote their testaments to the beyond. *Are these the Bitterroots?* we cried. *Or are we lost in Bathsheba's tent?* We would have moved into the trees, if we hadn't cut them down to smoke out that feverish band of men fingering compasses, parchment, and stones.

With so many books to read or burn, we could neither quench our thirst nor find the trail to the summit. The sign for *father* was impossible to learn; also *love*—a fence to approach with care, a land called Lot on our maps, the makers of which turned to salt before we looked and looked our empty gaze away. Only tongs would open our mouths and windows. And the blacksmith, the holy blacksmith was gone. Snakes coiled, like the woman writhing on the altar.

America? A world of swindling possibilities! the saint preached to the Great Invisibles, in the church ruins. His voice rang out over the mud walls and arches crumbling into saltbrush: *Only the ghosts of the gold panners know what I mean!* He fell to his knees, clutching a set of scales with which to weigh the nuggets of spirit unearthed by the flash flood which had carried away the altar and the pews. *Be fitful and moribund,* was his benediction. Then he dismissed the congregation he couldn't see— the higher beings who believed he was either a mayfly or a whale. They left without a word. And when he climbed the mountain behind the ruins, praying for a vision of paradise, he saw a train outrun its tracks and sink into sand.

We ran aground in a schooner named *Necessity*. And so close to shore! Our charts and compasses were useless; our flags sailed off in a gust of wind; our signal flares were words. Yet they lit up the night sky—at least those dark reaches containing ideas like *liberty* and *luck*. We couldn't find a way off the reef, and though waves battered the ship, splintering the unity that we had found in the course of our travels, still we had hope: a white flag to raise at daybreak, a message in a bottle for the scribe sewing his mouth shut at the bottom of the river.

Thieves swept through the foothills, the same men who campaigned against the canonization of the Great Auk and the grey wolf. They planned to loot the train carrying our dwindling resources: weed seeds, leashes, iron bars to drape across our windows. The engineers and passengers fled. Who could pass up the chance to spend forty days wandering in the desert? Not the saint, nor the thieves, nor even the navigator who fell asleep at our cry of *Land!*

Temptations everywhere: adders to set loose at the feast prepared for us by the natives, cacti to send to the botanist determined to restore the rain forest, fences to build around *The Pharmacy of God*. Railroad ties smoldered. Smoke laced with creosote engulfed us, preserving our vision of ourselves, even as we floated out to sea, clinging to pieces of the deck—the ship was gone. But we could see the mountain where the saint was counting the Great Invisibles assembling among the thieves. And the sky was ablaze with signs that no one could decipher. *Discovery* was the word burning the tips of our tongues. We learned it from the gold panners, not the messenger stitching memory up with words like *faith* and *father*.

What feathers song? the saint asked, measuring the waterfall, the volcanic cataract diverted by the thieves into the spa, where the Great Invisibles held court among the bathers. Farther along the ledge, at the entrance to the cave celebrated in local lore for the visions granted to its visitors, a woman picked through the bones of the hermits who inspired the saint to fast in spring. *What fathers our delight?* he called out. The woman looked away.

The mines were boarded up. Flocks of canaries circled the geysers in the slag heaps lining the mountain. The miners' ghosts prayed for a new Annunciation, an avalanche—anything to save the coach of the company football team, the driller who had lost his voice and memory in an explosion. The spray from the waterfall didn't scald the saint; absolution was out of the question. He might have been taking measurements for a bridal gown or a set of widow's weeds.

Steam and nooses everywhere, and no one to hide behind, no dress to tug or tar and feather. Silver bracelets kept disappearing from the shops. The only gold was blue—the sky, not the water draining from the locks behind the stadium, mixed with white paint. The barge stuck in the canal, loaded with hymnals for the pilgrims marching up the mountain, resembled an iceberg. Of course the nooses melted; the steam was only useful to the stamp collector who sent letters to the dead. The widow? She wore a turquoise dress two sizes too big for the woman who trained the canaries. She searched the spa for signs of the silversmith who had vanished in the desert.

In a geyser the saint heard ghosts counting silver and the saved. The waterfall was tall enough to house a miracle and wider than the future. What would be announced? Departure times for the missing miners: they never smelled the gas pooling in the chute. Birdcages floated downstream, whitened by the paint. A yellow dress hung from the ledge above the saint. *Angel,* he chanted.

The last prospectors built a fire under the gallows-tree, while the thieves forced water into the earth, poisoning the steam. No one could dissuade the widow from wearing a tourniquet to the evening service, not even the coach, whose frantic hand signals from the sideline recalled the glory of his youth. Snow clouds gathered overhead. Slag covered the new grass in the stadium. All the fathers would be there tonight, all the sons. Singing.

Limbs cracking in the orchard, and all our nets are torn, our dams and dumb-waiters clogged with silt and bursting open. Compose for the living a list of places to hide and send it to the dead: only they can keep your secret, the shape and color of the birthmark the priest peeled from your back, draped over the baptismal font, and blessed with incense, oil, and water from the burning river.

There must be music for this somewhere, even if the double rainbow burning through the scrolls destroyed our memory, our sense of measure. The rush on silver left us fitful and moribund. And we were too weak to forage for belief in the museum archives, too scared to hawk chickens in the square. A pity: a hungry crowd had assembled for the hanging of the clerk. But our timing was a long match that wouldn't light. Don't worry, no one will learn your name or why the sight of the scar still surprises you, the way sunlight dazzles a drunk lurching out of a bar late in the afternoon.

The apples rotting on the ground may explain why children are jumping from the trees, their screams a frozen river that no one skates across. Why the train left without us is another story, which cannot be told in daylight, not while the dead polish the silver with flames invisible to the living. All around us the dead are working to reveal the luster of *the language of flesh and roses* passed down in fragments by Assyrian scribes—a language we never learned. We were too busy writing the last wills and testaments of our enemies: a series of adventurous erotic works to bury in the orchard.

Don't ring the bell again unless you are prepared to answer for the clerk climbing the gallows. Tell us instead why the saint fled at our approach—and where you hid him during the miners' uprising, after the vision vouchsafed to him proved false. In the dumbwaiter are directions to the safe houses burned after the first clash. The traps set in the museum for the bear that wrecked the beehives won't work until the philosophers of desire renew their licenses to interpret dreams.

The Great Invisibles must translate the smoke signals spiraling above the mountain, or else we may mistake the church ruins for railroad tracks. The silver is gone, but nets rise from the depths of the reservoir into the sky, with a catch of words and fictions unbearable to utter—and that is why the dam is falling down, falling down. The clerk's crime? Keeping a ledger of that catch.

Who will inherit your tattoos, the stars and snakes covering your back? What name will you use to cross the border closed for the execution? Will you meet the hangman? The saint? The match we called rhythm became our style: it burned the papers of the scribe who scanned the heavens for a language elastic enough to light the objects of his desire—the steppe, the bell, the trap.

Sharpen your skates: the ice is hardening in your voice, black ice through which we can see into the molten core of the earth. This is no time to listen to the choir singing hosannas from the riverbank, not with a moat of flaming oil engulfing the fortress. Better to practice school figures than report the woman stealing flowers from a grave: figure eights instead of fingerprints.

Clean linens are in the archives watched over by the museum guard. On Judgment Day the key he buried in the orchard will be unearthed, and white sheets will swaddle the world. Meantime you should set up camp on the steppe and try to sleep. A bell will summon you to the execution.

The clerk wants bagpipes played at his funeral, not trumpets and zithers. No one must attend the exhibition he curated before he was condemned, charring the scrolls for our viewing pleasure. Threshed by the Great Invisibles, those grains belong to memory and desire; the husks are for the spangled dead who reek of silver polish; the silos are packed with fathers smoking in the dark.

Flesh and roses? A fragment entrusted to a minor bard, who broke the tablet on a train and never learned another word of that language. *That's one way to avoid the hangman,* said the museum guard who won the singing contest: his voice was the loudest of all! And it was his idea to pluck the chickens in the darkroom, then feed them photographs of concentration camps to ease their skittishness before placing them in the dumbwaiter, which is also falling down.

Drunk on the prospect of the future, we could hail a notary and sign away our vision of the past—priests displaying strips of skin in church, children girdling trees, the clerk's last speech... Or should we say: *The granaries are filled with names and fingerprints. In the new exhibit a stuffed bear hovers over the trap, with a rose in its teeth. The noose is bigger than we thought.*

How will the Great Invisibles prepare us for Judgment Day? If only they had left instructions—

Choose a warm page from *The History of the World* to lead you across the frozen strait that linked the nomads to the needleworkers; the rainstorm ushering in the Flood to recite a rough draft of *Metamorphoses* to the Minister of Desire; a slow day at the crematorium to burn your unopened letters from the dead.

Write up the dreams of everyone in the crowd by the gallows-tree and send them to the condemned man's children: an almanac of prophesies no one should ignore.

Learn which words will take you directly to the front lines at Ardennes, which will let you return from battle with the Persians in the caravan of the wounded, and which will spirit you out of Bathsheba's tent ahead of the duplicitous king.

Canonize those who make pilgrimages into the marvelous archives of chance!

Tickle the tyrant before he goes to bed, and as he falls asleep read to him the list of casualties from his endless war on memory and desire: alms and alchemy, faith healing and fictions—the molten dreams that erupted from deep within the earth, surged upward through the sea, and floated toward the sky, settling into the constellations that guide mariners, lovers, and scribes through the night.

On the day before the saint's election into eternal life, mount a dark horse raised on the steppe, ride from one voting booth to another in the City of God, shouting, *Marco Polo!*, and declare yourself the winner of the benefit race, organized by the luckless angel, the Angel of Dust, to resurrect the art of friendship.

Listen for the train whistle in the highest pitch of the pipe organ played by the miner's widow, then circle the church ruins, crying, *All aboard!*

No one will make it across the border, despite the hangman's promise to free the Assyrians inscribed in the tablets, the singers praised by the ancients. The philosophers of desire, haunted by the specter of the fortress above the frozen river, are planning their escape from the claims of memory. Nor will they leave instructions for interpreting the dreams that guide the once and future rioters—the scribes—through the labyrinth of ashes the dead construct each night.

How hard you tried to prove the flowers belonged to you, not to the actor buried in the nude, the shade caught in a costume change! Even the grave robbers were impressed. But your aliases didn't fool the Great Invisibles: your fingerprints were on the clerk's ledger. His tombstone, too. *Where did you hide his body?* cried his children. *Who tied the noose? Who claimed his legacy?*

The flames in the moat rose higher than the price of silver, higher even than the waves that washed over the island forming out at sea and swamped the schooner called *Necessity.* We clung to it, as if it were our name, when the volcano erupted! Lava flowed into our music, carving out time signatures we couldn't play on our trumpets and zithers, not without destroying our lips and fingers, our style: wounds to measure and dress with saltwater. It was then that the soldiers hidden in the woods beyond the moat recorded the names they knew you by: *History, Memory, Desire.*

Bells rang late into the night, signaling the end of the public hangings, though only the fathers knew who would escape their sons' decrees to build more dams and concentration camps. Why didn't we heed the clerk's warnings about the silt collecting in our veins and reservoirs? Or bury the scrolls entrusted to us? Or avoid the traps set for the bear?

We thought the museum would never close. And the guard assured us that he could decipher the tablets in time for the opening of the exhibit of photographs from Ardennes: prints steeped in poison gas, busts wrapped in bandages torn from the wounded, blank canvases titled *The Beginning* and *The End*. We couldn't wait to see them! The catalogue of losses was exquisite. And the churches packed with canisters of cyanide were *lovely, dark and deep*. In *The History of the World* the trains were leaving for the last page, a station named *Desire*. Our gloves and masks fit perfectly.

No need to be surprised by the coming floods. Nor should you imagine you will be saved: nets may swirl around you, offering fictions anyone might believe (*the sea will give up her dead!*), and still you will drag us under. For our plan to seduce the hanging judges was ill-conceived: our spins and pirouettes, the little flourishes we executed to close the program, hastened our demise. They granted clemency only to the woman in the skin-toned bodysuit. Her skates were rusted, her voice a bucket dipped in the well of the deserted fortress; her farewell speech, delivered as she climbed down from the gallows-tree, quenched our thirst—and then she vanished from sight. Smoke was our reward for listening to the soldiers' stories about you.

The hairless men in saffron robes burning themselves alive—we had no language with which to shield them from the saint's wrath and nowhere to hide the roses they tossed to us as the flames consumed them. *Was that part of the routine?* we asked the fallen skaters when they took their places among the martyrs in the square. *To caress the ice with arabesques until gravity betrayed you, and then glide away from us?* Their artistic score was the match the last monk lit for them. *Ten, nine, eight,* said the soldiers in the soot, clicking beads and bullets, dreaming of snakes—and knives, forged in the stars, with which to hack them up.

The border patrol reported hundreds of sheets drying in the river willows, curtains rising in the church ruins, horses escaped from the corral of a tyrant's sleep and approaching from the steppe. The museum guard sent us the messages that he was saving for confession: *Clean the chimney before you burn your last will and testament! Sanctify the dying apple trees and seal their girdled trunks with incense! Bless the waiter who brought you charm instead of change!*

Dusk. The singers, opening their mouths, turned to stone. Lost in a maze of ash-blonde hair, we followed the thread called *Desire*, and long before we reached the border, where coiling snakes hissed and no bells tolled, we realized that the judges had revised *The History of the World* under the merciless gaze of the saint. Drunk on your name, on the tattoos we knew you by, the signs which the Great Invisibles had vouchsafed to you before we went to sea, we could almost understand what the singers wanted to tell us; why that thread might lead us back to you, to land, to memory; and how the tablets crumbling in our hands might save us in the end.

III

Neither traitor, nor perjurer, the exile whispered from the witness stand. But it was time to remodel the courthouse, and his diplomatic skills were no longer needed, argued the museum guard responsible for the welfare of the missing judges. He blocked the door to the chambers in which negotiations had broken down between the warring factions—the men with sickles and the men without. The bus to the stadium was crowded with birdwatchers, jurors called to the tribunal of the wild. No one could say what had become of the court reporter.

The next battlefield? Architects from Assyria surrounded the new airport, demanding action on their blueprints for the future—a future of wooden shoes and vigils on the loading ramp for the hereafter. The directions were hidden centuries ago, in the last stall of the covered bazaar, where the rug merchants were rewriting the penal code, reversing the practice of the clerics. Sabbaths would go the way of the saber-toothed tiger. The punishment for browsing would be severe: the loss of the right hand. And it was too late to change the flight plan of the pilgrims en route to the past. Nor could they hope to receive a fair trial there, not even if the missing judges turned up.

Fences were falling everywhere, spurring the migration of refugees, caribou, and currency. It was herding time: shepherds rounded up sacks of gold and silver and set them in the fold, then drove out the last victims of the war—acolytes converted into money-changers, gunrunners blistered by the sun, glass blowers who cut the throats of the white horses galloping in moonlight, sheep hungering for the hides of wolves, books that could burn a forest down... Armed with posthole diggers and rolls of barbed wire, animal trainers headed for the border, where the refugees awaiting their instructions were the first to see the hourglass registering changes in the weather.

How to solve the Bikini problem—the contaminated atoll, not advances in women's fashions? *Pensions!* cried the old men marching on the courthouse. *More and more!* was the slogan printed on their sandwich boards. The topless women sprawling on the steps chanted *Less and less!* Who was telling the truth? The museum guard boarded up the windows overlooking the square, ignoring the exile's plea to weigh the testimony of his senses. Shoemakers took measurements in the street, woodcutters sharpened their axes, merchants noted a surge in the sale of votive candles. The women's breasts were burning in the sun. Everything tasted like the end.

A plane circled the airport, dumping fuel. Draftsmen lit matches to read the specifications for the control tower. The landing lights offered alternate versions of the past and future, according to a poll taken by the flight attendants, who were happiest in the air—e.g., the present. They urged the pilot to fly on: *Circle globes, not graveyards!* They thumbed through their guidebooks when the plane stalled. The passengers—pilgrims condemned to wandering, judges undone by their reliance on precedent in matters of the heart—put their heads between their legs, praying that the landing lights were stars. The pilot radioed the navigators sequestered in the Tower of Babel. White noise was their reply. The plane spun toward the unborn. The fight attendants waved.

In the stadium, before the birdwatchers settled into their seats, thousands of nesting swans took flight and, flapping their heavy wings, darkened the sky. The transcripts from the trial were burning in the woods. The court reporter was rumored to be hiding in Assyria. Nevertheless the jurors had reached a verdict: the birds had to go. The architects thus unrolled a hundred Persian rugs over the grass, nests, and eggs, marking the boundaries of the arena in which the one-eyed and the blind would fight it out. The swans flew toward the blazing trees. Smoke rose from the pages of the warriors' life lists. The jurors waited for the games to begin.

The exile concluded his testimony with a praise song for the concerto dedicated to the Emperor of Necessity, the slow movement of which evoked an archipelago of royal palms and rubber trees, of sun gods and salt marshes, of libations to childhood and the milky gaze of the leper who dragged himself down to the harbor to watch the debt-ridden family board a ship bound for the capital of the world... And the cadenzas written in a variable key evoked for him the specter of History, *the renewer of all things,* which drove him from his homeland, across the steppe, into the annals of rain and wind and snow: rooms in which no one ever spoke again.

When the courtroom emptied, the exile set sail on an ark of language, counting off the animals that fed on his imagination—horses and parrots and feral cats. When he looked away, the deckhands dropped the crate containing his library overboard, then hid the crate among the barrels of salted meat. O brine-soaked words stowed in memory's hold! O folios reeking of the coming war! O music for the last days! The books rotted through before the ship made landfall. And on the first page of the sea the exile began to write.

The sentences handed down, in absentia, inspired the pilgrims to turn the tribunal of the wild into a prison short on beds for the inmates. They claimed to know the lunar phases of eternity, they condemned the Great Auk to the high seas of History, the saber-toothed tiger to hunting on a savanna cleared of prey, the white wolf to howling at the new moon. Smoke plumed above the hives of words the exile kept in the orchard. Honey bees swarmed around the stump of a tree felled at the start of the war. The swans returned to the burning river. How to reduce the prison population without releasing the damned or inciting a riot among the saved: this was the dilemma. The sentences? Hard labor for the faithful, grace for the migrants, and for the exile, immortality.

Fresh from the leper colony, the court reporter needed new tools—a miner's lamp and shears, a sextant and a rhyming dictionary—to determine who spiked the punch at the exile's wedding of mythology and music: a ceremony without witnesses, performed for the ages—the court reporter, that is, the errant scribe. She had gone off in search of Assyria and in a dream discovered a route to Atlantis, only to forget her vision the next morning. *Here comes the bride*, she whispered to her drunken chauffeur, the stowaway she rescued from the irradiated island. He said the punch glowed in the dark. She told him to drive to the airport. She wanted gold, cashmere, the rights to the memoirs of those trapped in the Tower of Babel, and rhymes—directions—for the future. *Keep your eyes on the word*, she ordered, steering around the commandment to peel the scales from her enemy's eyes and skin. *The groom's the guilty party here.*

The exile, blindfolded and swaying in the great winds of the future, walked the plank to find *the honor of the Sea*, the tides by which he might be known, and pledged allegiance to the waves swelling with the separate languages of mariners and memory, bells and birds of passage. The past was in revolt: the salt caverns flooded, a sea rose where the forest had burned down, nothing would sink until the new moon drifted through the final phase of History, tugging planes out of the sky and into the waters swirling around the charred stumps, the reef on which the exile washed up, under *the shadow of a great bird.* There he glimpsed eternity, in whirlwinds and waterspouts and the drowned. How the wings glittered in the prism of the glass blowers' boat! How the last tourists, the sun-blistered gunrunners, loved their journey to the end!

There were not enough sickles to prevent another war between the one-armed rug collectors from Babylon and the flight crew lost in the Trinity Alps. Nor was the thread in the bank vault strong enough to mend the raveling of belief or halt the erosion of the coastline. And the jurors counting the heads propped on the pikes of the warriors unwilling to leave the stadium could not reach a verdict in the trial of the unborn. The pilgrims refused to measure the flames ebbing and flowing through the pages of the exile's testimony. The missing judges had no blueprints for the afterlife. And who would welcome the next wave of refugees—the money-changers and glass blowers, woodcutters and candlers from the leper colony? Yet we vowed to follow the thread through the labyrinth of convictions alien to our own until we emerged, at daybreak, from the last, the darkest, volume of History, speaking in tongues.

One man, one vote, once, declared the old men at the courthouse, the ones who razed the exile's flat and set fire to his manuscripts. *Be fruitful and multiply,* sang the topless women destined for the stocks, the pioneering souls who might have saved the white horses bleeding by the fence. The exile praised the following: Robinson Crusoe, rains, winds, snows, seamarks, birds, drought, and night. On the horizon was a strange glow. The old men tallied up their ballots and elected to serve the Emperor of Necessity. The women were dragged into the courtroom, where the exile was extolling their virtues to the architects. Soon there would be laws to stop him—laws that he would break. For he knew it was *enough to be the guilty conscience of his time.*

The sentries ignored the candles burning along the river. And the swans did not return to their nests, because we were preening in the Tower of Babel, clucking like hens in a slaughterhouse. The navigators slept. The pilgrims fled before the lepers entered the stadium. No one was confused about the order of succession. Runners swarmed the roads and bridges, each carrying a torch for the unborn, a changing key; from the mountaintop it looked as if the city was on fire. Every block had its own radio station; ham operators transmitted around the clock: nothing could penetrate the airwaves. *White Noise* was what we called this tribunal of the wild, the transcript of which we dared not publish. So we fired the court reporter. Her severance pay? A starter's pistol. The runners took their marks. *Birds,* sang the exile, *lances lifted at all the frontiers...* Go!

Christopher Merrill is the author of five books of poetry, including *Watch Fire*, for which he received the Lavan Younger Poets Award from the Academy of American Poets; many books of translations and edited volumes; and five works of nonfiction, among them, *Only the Nails Remain: Scenes from the Balkan Wars*, *Things of the Hidden God: Journey to the Holy Mountain*, and *The Tree of the Doves: Ceremony, Expedition, War*. His writings have been translated into twenty-five languages; his journalism appears in a variety of publications; his honors include a knighthood in arts and letters from the French government. He directs the International Writing Program at the University of Iowa.

Author photograph by Ram Devineni.